A STUDENT'S GUIDE TO OPEN LEARNING

MOYA DAVIS

First edition 1993
Reprinted 1994; Reprinted with minor amendments 1997
Reprinted 1998, 2000

Published by
Emap Healthcare Open Learning
Emap Healthcare Ltd
Greater London House
Hampstead Road
London NW1 7EJ

Companies and representatives throughout the world

Printed in Great Britain by
Drogher Press
Christchurch
Dorset

ISBN 1–902499–25–5

Editorial team

Patsy Dale, chief sub-editor, Emap Healthcare Open Learning
Cathy Hull, head of curriculum development and publishing,
 Emap Healthcare Open Learning (commissioning editor)
Ann Mroz, sub-editor
Gareth Renowden, publishing consultant, copy editor
Destine Simon, projects manager

Contents

Introduction

If you are thinking about studying, you may be considering an open learning course. Although the term 'open learning' is widely used, there is considerable misunderstanding about what it actually means, and how students can benefit fully from its use. This book has been written to help you decide if open learning is for you, and, if you decide it is, to help you get the most from your studies.

The book has six chapters :

Chapter 1: Being an open learner explains the term 'open' and 'distance' learning. Possible differences between school-age and adult learners are explored, and the relationship between independent learners and their tutors is discussed.

Chapter 2: Getting started considers different ways of assessing where you stand when beginning a course of study. The development of a personal profile combined with individual goal-setting is explained.

Chapter 3: Study skills helps you to make the most of study by managing your study schedule and time using libraries and reading effectively, learning to analyse written and oral arguments critically, and keeping useful study notes.

Chapter 4: Charting progress suggests creative ways in which you can use a reflective diary to chart your academic, personal and professional growth.

Chapter 5: Making the best of assessment considers constructive approaches to providing yourself and others with evidence of your progress. How to use individual performance review to your advantage, and ways of developing skills necessary for project work, essay writing and formal examinations are described.

Chapter 6: Evaluating the experience helps you to review your study diary and reassess goals positively. This chapter helps you to give useful feedback to others concerned with your learning, be they college principals, tutors, mentors or colleagues.

1: Being an open learner

IN THIS CHAPTER WE SHALL:

- **Describe distance learning and open learning**
- **Discuss the advantage of being an independent learner**
- **Discuss the relationship between you and your open learning tutor**

What is open learning?

Have you got an open mind? Having an open mind means being ready to consider new ideas and experiences. A closed mind is resistant to different views or opinions. The words 'open' and 'closed' are used very similarly to describe different approaches to education.

Open and closed philosophies of education

An open philosophy of education aims to remove as many barriers to learning as possible, opening up opportunities for learning.

This means that it concentrates on your needs as a student rather than on the needs of your employers or of society in general. You are at the centre of the educational process and in control of it, instead of being on the receiving end of what others feel should be provided. Open education is 'learner centred'[1]. An open philosophy of learning allows you to study what you wish, when, where and how you wish. Although it may be necessary for others to assess your progress, for example where a course leads to a qualification, your own assessment of learning is vital. The learning which results from an open philosophy of education is very appropriately termed *open learning*.

'Closed' educational philosophies aim to develop specific knowledge or skills, usually to enable students to carry out particular activities. This can be an essential approach in some instances, but there can be drawbacks. Closed philosophies do not encourage questioning approaches. This can limit creativity and allow bad practice to continue unchallenged. Self-assessment is not usually built into such courses, and students are sometimes left feeling that it is only learning that is of importance to the institution that is recognised, not learning that is of value to them.

Openness and closure are, however, two opposite ends of a path running from complete closure to complete openness and courses can be developed anywhere between the two extremes.

Different ways of planning courses

Because study based on a closed philosophy will be tightly controlled, you can be given a very detailed description of the things you are expected to have learnt or achieved when you have finished studying. A course which does this is said to have an *objectives curriculum* and the stated outcomes are called 'learning objectives'.

For example, if you were taking a course on visual handicap you might be given a list of learning objectives that includes one which states that at the end of the course you should be able to :

'Define myopia, hypermetropia, astigmatism, and presbyopia'.

Many open courses can also state learning outcomes, but they may be less strictly defined. An example of a broader learning outcome is that you should be able to:

'Appreciate the increasing problem of visual impairment in our ageing society'.

Study based on an open philosophy may be developed using a *process curriculum*. Such courses do not prescribe learning outcomes. They offer you learning opportunities to explore, rather than specified skills to be developed or knowledge to be acquired. When courses offer a learning process which can deliver different benefits to different students, learning outcomes set by anyone other than each student would be of limited use.

Courses like this are often described as *process driven* because it is you, the individual, who identifies personal learning outcomes to be achieved by using the learning opportunities offered by the course. You are in the driving seat.

'Face-to-face' and 'distance' methods in education

Most of us have a great deal of experience of conventional methods of education in which teacher and learners work together face-to-face. Children spend most of their school days in classrooms and many adults take courses during which they spend most of their study time in lectures and seminars.

Distance education is a way of providing teaching, and bringing about learning, when the teacher and the student are separated[2].

The separation does not have to be great. You and your tutor can be in the same geographical location. On the other hand, the separation could be vast, with your tutor many hundreds of miles away from you. In either case the usual forms of communication and teaching that take place in a classroom must be replaced by other methods. Distance education therefore uses a variety of means to communicate with students, including:

• Text in all forms, such as books; articles; specially written study materials
• Audio tapes
• Radio
• Slides
• Video
• Television.

The distance method of education often involves the use of study *exercises* or *activities* which suggest that you undertake particular tasks. These encourage students to interact with the study materials and take the place of the questions and discussions which flesh and blood tutors often have with their classes. Exercises may vary from very simple tasks such as:

Find out about the advocacy services offered by Age Concern in your area, or find out if there is a voluntary organisation in your own particular field of work which offers advocacy services. A good starting point for this would be a directory of voluntary organisations in your local library[3].

to complex analysis such as

Think about where you grew up and make some notes about the sort of community you grew up in. By community we mean the

Cont...

...cont

people you grew up with, played with, went to school with, and their families. Describe the attitudes of this community towards:

Children	**Divorce**
Old people	**Marriage**
Work	**People from other cultures**
Sex	**Religion**
Death	**Illness**
Unmarried mothers	**Health**
Working mothers	**Handicap**

Write a sentence or two in your diary about each. Remember to write in the part of your diary which is confidential[4].

Both these examples are from the Emap Healthcare Open Learning Enrolled Nurse Conversion Programme. In distance learning, each Activity, whether simple or complex, is followed by feedback to reassure you that the work you have done has been useful to the learning process.

Distance method and open learning

Combining distance method with open learning offers access to study which can be undertaken when and where it suits you. Because it is student-centred, many adults find its approach to education more suited to their needs than conventional day-release or full-time courses. Where learning objectives are used, they are likely to be relatively broad. Frequently, however, intended outcomes are identified by each student in a process of personal profiling and goal-setting which we shall discuss in Chapter 2.

When open philosophies are combined with the distance method, it is possible to offer a very broad range of learning opportunities through the exercises. These may ask you to read, reflect, inquire, write or carry out a wide variety of Activities. Commonly used types of Activity assist in:

Building a knowledge base: you are asked to read a piece of factual material and to extract important points. The feedback is likely to list the vital points that you should have identified so that you can check this new knowledge.

Undertaking critical analysis and appraisal: the study materials may cover opposing beliefs and arguments to stimulate a debate in your mind. The subsequent Activity might ask you to write a short analysis of the arguments. The feedback provides you with a résumé of the main points which could have been made, highlighting areas where your own arguments might have been included.

Applying theory to real life: you are asked to consider a range of ideas, opinions or research findings. The resulting Activity suggests that you reflect on these items in relation to personal experience. The feedback may suggest follow-up action to provide you with other opinions about the real-life situation. In this way you are never left asking 'So what?' or feeling emotionally vulnerable.

Examining attitudes and emotions: the materials may provide examples of opposing attitudes and ask you to identify your own feelings. Distance learning has great advantages here because it is easier to admit to having attitudes others think unacceptable if we are free to be totally open with ourselves. For example, a prejudice against male midwives might be easier to face up to if we are alone at home than if we are in a professional nursing group. That openness could be the start of getting rid of our prejudice. If we decide to share our learning it is often easier to have our attitudes and prejudices challenged by family or friends, instead of by colleagues such as line managers or tutors. Feedback following this sort of Activity might debate the reasons why individuals hold opinions which they find difficult to acknowledge.

Quality in open learning

If you are going to commit time and money to studying by open learning you need to be sure that you are investing in good courses or materials that meet your needs. The library of your local further or higher education college, or your professional library, is likely to have examples of open learning materials and may give you the opportunity to examine them. Points to consider are:

- The range of subjects that can be studied

- The different academic levels that are catered for

- The varying length of courses

- The variety of interactive exercises and activities offered

- The degree of closure and openness

- Whether the particular style used appeals to you.

Credible open learning provision should:

- Help you to achieve what you want to achieve. You should always ask: 'Is this the right course of study for me? Does it use the most appropriate method, with the right degree of tutorial support, to meet my current learning needs?'

- Provide evidence that materials have been developed by credible educationists and fully tested by students during development

- Have the backing of a respected educational or professional organisation to enable you to gain academic or professional credit for your studies when appropriate.

Organisations producing such materials include:
- The Open University
- The Distance Learning Centre, South Bank University
- Emap Healthcare Open Learning.

A guide providing an extensive list of producers of open learning materials is now available[5].

Are adult learners different?

If you are asked to imagine a 'studying scene', as if in a play, what would come into your mind? In such a situation most of us will fall back on previous experience, so you will have been unusual if your 'studying scene' did not relate to an earlier occasion when you were hoping to learn. We rarely approach learning with a clean slate because there is always some previous knowledge or experience to influence our actions. Of course, this frequently works to our advantage, because as we progress through life we have more knowledge and experience to draw on.

The knowledge that we possess has often been hard earned in formal learning situations. Most of us have spent hours trying to commit to memory lists of facts, such as the positions of individual bones. This may have been essential learning if our professional lives, and the safety of our clients, depended upon our anatomical knowledge. This type of learning relies more on memory than on understanding. There is a strong argument that understanding is of far greater value than simple retention of facts. It is by relating essential knowledge to experience that we learn most effectively.

Learning which results from experience is called *experiential learning* and we frequently use it to understand why people feel and behave in particular ways. This is another reason why open learning is particularly suitable for adults. Open philosophies value, and build on, the knowledge and experience that each of us brings to the learning process. Open learning activities are designed to offer learning opportunities that take the personal, and, where appropriate, professional, experience of each learner into account.

This can be done in a conventional course, where students and tutors are face-to-face. Open discussion among the group can be a part of such courses, and is a valuable combination of an open philosophy and conventional teaching methods. However, combining distance methods with open learning offers many people a greater opportunity for truly student-centred, independent learning.

Independent students and their tutors

It is perfectly possible to produce study materials that can be used by individuals without tutorial support. If study materials were designed so that they could be used only with a tutor, many people who might otherwise use them would be denied educational opportunities. However, there is considerable evidence that people are more successful studying at a distance if there is some form of tutorial support[6]. Additionally, if study is intended to result in an academic or other qualification, the tutor is likely to be involved in assessment.

An equal partnership

Because we always use previous experience when coping with new situations, it is very easy for mature students to assume a childhood 'pupil' role when dealing with their tutor. Here is one such student's experience:

Jane is 28 years old and works as a manager in a unit with 30 staff. She is intelligent and articulate, is already well qualified both academically and professionally, and manages her unit effectively and confidently. Having recently started an open learning course, Jane found that because of pressure of work she could not attend the first tutorial.

Cont...

Over the next week she became convinced that the tutor would mark her down as an uncommitted student, and she could not bring herself to start studying. Finally, after some badgering from her boyfriend — who pointed out that no one who had paid several hundred pounds for a course could be considered not to be committed to it — Jane rang her tutor. When she explained what had happened and apologised, the tutor told her that she was not alone in missing the tutorial.

The tutor explained that open learning was designed to provide access to education for people who had exactly the sorts of difficulties that Jane was experiencing. Jane's stress levels were reduced immediately. When she sat back and thought about it she realised that her panic was a response to punishments she remembered from her school days.

In an opening learning course, your tutor is there to help you to learn in whatever way suits you best: you and your tutor are equal partners, with your tutor supporting the learning. Although tutors may offer a range of tutorials, seminars and other teaching sessions — and many students do find these invaluable — there should be no rigid requirement for students to attend.

Communication between tutors and students

Because open learning tutors provide a support system for students, they need to offer a variety of ways of keeping in touch. These include written communication, telephone communication and attendance at tutorials. We will discuss these in Chapter 3.

You are in charge

As an open learning student you are in charge of your own studies. Although an assessment scheme may be imposed for very positive reasons, such as enabling you to gain academic or professional qualifications, an open learning programme will also enable you to meet your own needs. Although most of us value the opportunity for doing this, it can also feel overwhelming and daunting. This is particularly true if all of our previous experiences of education have been based upon being told what and how to learn. It is therefore important when you begin studying that you spend time thinking about what kind of learner you are, how you learn best and what motivates you to learn. We shall be considering some of these factors in the next chapter.

Where you achieve learning that is not acknowledged by the assessment scheme, open learning should help you to assess and acknowledge the additional learning for yourself. Chapter 2, 'Getting started', also helps you lay the foundations for this process.

2: Getting started

IN THIS CHAPTER WE SHALL:

- **Discuss ways in which self-awareness can help you to learn**
- **Describe how you can use profiling to produce an accurate assessment of yourself**
- **Explain the value of goal-setting in the learning process**

By this stage you may well have a general idea of what you want to learn and have decided to give open learning a chance. One of the main advantages of open learning is that you can select courses or, by using mix-and-match modules, you can build yourself a course that suits your needs. In addition, you can spend more time on subjects that interest you and less on areas with which you are already familiar. As a potential open learning student you therefore have to ask: 'Where do I start?' The obvious answer is that it depends on the knowledge and skills that you already have, but you may need some help in identifying them.

Self-awareness

Probably the most accurate way for people to assess their strengths and weaknesses is to develop self-awareness. Some use the term 'self-awareness' critically, suggesting that it means being self-centred. This is far from the truth, especially when it is used to describe a process in which individuals develop accurate pictures of their knowledge and skills. Once we have this picture we can plan to build on our strengths and to put in some work on our weaknesses.

There are a number of ways of doing this, the simplest being to sit down and list the things we think we know and the skills we think we have. That is not a systematic appraisal and can, at times, be a very hit and miss affair. Additionally, such an 'off-the-cuff' exercise can be heavily influenced by comments made by others, often at very early stages of our lives. Here is Mary's experience:

I was the only girl in the family and whenever visitors asked about our progress at school they were told: 'Well of course, Peter is absolutely brilliant, and David does very well considering the time he has had away from school with his chest. Mary? She's not academic but she's very artistic.'

For years I assumed that this was true and never bothered with any study at school, convinced that it would be a waste of time. I thought those in my professional training who told me I was intelligent were being kind, and even when I came top in tests I simply thought the others must be even dimmer than I was. It took a number of years, and many exam successes, before I began to think that perhaps I was not stupid after all.

Many people have been incorrectly labelled by their families or teachers. Others have had their learning limited because there was no educational provision available. Lacking opportunities to learn, such people have never found the true extent of their abilities. Open learning, using distance methods, offers ways of remedying such deficits.

Personal profiling

Personal profiling is a process in which you systematically review every aspect of your life, noting down aptitudes, skills and achievements to build up a rounded picture of the person you really are. Profiling will help you to identify goals to be met, to chart your progress and record achievements. Profiling can seem time-consuming, but it nearly always saves time in the end. It helps you to identify the most profitable areas to spend time and effort on. For this reason you should begin your personal profiling before you make a commitment to a particular course of study. It is also an ongoing process, something you should repeat and build upon, and we shall return to this aspect in Chapter 6. 'Evaluating the experience'. Because some of the reflections will be very personal, you should keep most of the profile confidential, unless you choose to share your reflections with others.

A profile will usually include a review, a diary, and a personal and professional profile. The review may be divided into a number of sections, each highlighting different aspects of your life. For example the Emap Healthcare Open Learning *Profile Pack*[7] has eight sections.

Section 1: Your working life

A long hard look at your career pattern can help to identify strengths or interests that have proved fruitful, and perhaps to pinpoint some which you have not yet fully utilised. As part of this process, profiling helps you to produce a professional record, detailing employment dates and other information.

This part of profiling can help in planning your future career development and in applying for new posts or avenues of study. Profiling is not simply a historical record. It is central to continuing personal and job-related education and growth.

Section 2: Your life and times

This section of the review is designed to help you to record and reflect on major experiences in your life. It gives you an opportunity to think about important occasions, relationships and experiences by creating a diagram or picture of your life — a 'lifeline'. It is likely that had Mary, whose incorrect childhood 'labelling' we have described, completed this sort of review, she would have realised that simply gaining a place at a secondary school by passing exams must have indicated that she was academic, whatever her parents told people! Many people completing this section gain startling insights into ways in which other people's opinions have influenced their lives. With that insight, they are able to reassess their abilities and move forward. You may be the same.

Section 3: Values, attitudes and beliefs

These vital factors affect our personal and professional lives and our relationships with others, but they are not always easy to recognise. The Activities in this section help you to identify your main values and beliefs, your personal qualities and the people who have significantly influenced you.

Ben was 28 and was being pushed by his health-care manager to study for a management degree and to apply for promotion. When he completed this section of his profile he concluded that the thing he most valued was helping other people to recover from illness. He admired people who quietly worked away to help others and felt he had been particularly influenced during his training by an older colleague who had repeatedly told him: 'It's the small things that make each day bearable or otherwise for the people we care for, not the earth-shattering events.' This had been underlined by the experience of seeing a patient who had not got the meal he had ordered getting in a temper and collapsing. Lack of attention to seemingly unimportant things by someone else had resulted in that person's death.

When he completed this section of the review, Ben concluded that taking his manager's advice and studying management would be wrong for him. Instead, he began looking for a course in advanced clinical studies which would allow him to develop his professional knowledge and skills and remain in a practice setting.

Section 4: What kind of learner are you?

In this section you are encouraged to review your past learning experiences, both good and bad. You may discover that bad experiences were caused by an inappropriate learning style being forced upon you.

> Derek learns best by debate, but some years ago he went on a course where the tutor always liked to 'win' and ridiculed students who disagreed with her. Derek felt mortified by this and decided that in future he would not voice his own opinions.

Profiling his learning style would help Derek to reassess this bad experience, perhaps working out ways to have dealt with that particular tutor more effectively. He could also review subsequent learning and be encouraged to return to his former active learning style.

Section 5: The skills inventory

In this section, you explore the unique combination of skills and competences that you possess. There are seven categories in this section of the Profile Pack Review:

- Communication and personal skills

- Planning and observation

- Management skills

- Aspects of teamwork

- Practical dexterity

- Study, research and knowledge

- Self-awareness and reflection.

You rate each skill or competence on a scale from one to six. You can feel confidence in those that score well and clearly identify those which you may need to develop further.

Section 6: Focus on achievement

It is a sad fact of life for many of us that we remember, and often repeatedly agonise over, those things that have not gone according to our hopes or plans. We sometimes cast aside or explain away successes. This is what Mary had initially done with her early professional successes by putting them down to her fellow students being 'even dimmer' than she thought she was herself.

It is, therefore, good to have an opportunity to set the record straight, by reflecting on your successes. You are encouraged to ask the questions:

• What went well?

• Why was it a success?

• Which particular personal skills or qualities made it a success?

• How could it have gone even better?

• Which additional skills would have been useful?

This sort of incident analysis is, however, more than a way of making you feel good. It is part of the process of identifying overall strengths and weaknessess and mapping out action for the future. Because it does this, 'focusing' on achievement should become a regular activity for all of us.

Section 7: The review summary

The purpose of this section if to summarise the strengths you have identified in the previous sections and to highlight areas for development. You are asked to complete a review summary sheet which, unlike the other review material, may be looked at by other people, either in informal discussion or as part of a performance review.

Section 8: Setting goals

Once you have identified areas for development, you need to decide exactly where you want to go in the learning process, how you might get there and how you will be sure that you have arrived where you want to be. That means setting goals. It is not a completed process, but it does need to be clearly understood and carried out well, which is why we are devoting the next part of this chapter to describing it in detail.

Goal-setting

The terms 'goal' and 'objective' are often used interchangeably. They can also be used to indicate different levels of a process of working towards targets. Because these words are used in a variety of ways, it is sensible always to establish their use in each context. We are using the word 'goal' here in the simple sense of a target set by an individual for his or her own personal and professional development. A 'goal' as used here is something you intend to work towards and achieve.

An example of a personal goal could be:

'Learn to speak sufficient French to enable me to buy food in small French shops'.

We can call that our 'goal statement'. Fine, but by when will we learn to speak French, and by what means and how well will we learn to speak it?

Simply saying what we intend to do — making a goal statement — is not enough because we would then have an open-ended goal of learning to speak French 'sometime'. The goal would also be open-ended because we have not specified how we hope to learn French, our plan of action, what courses, teachers, programmes, tapes or any other means of learning French we intend to use. We must also set some sort of standard or have some criteria for our ability to speak French, or we could say we have achieved the goal after our first purchase — even if it was made with considerable use of sign language and very little spoken French at all.

Goals must therefore have:

- A clear goal statement with a timescale

- Criteria for success in achieving the goal

- A plan of action you intend to take to work towards achieving the goal — an 'action plan'.

Our example of the 'learn to speak French' goal would then become:

Goal statement with timescale: 'Learn to speak sufficient French by my holiday next June to enable me to buy food in small French shops.'

Criteria for success: I will assess that I can:

'Ask for items without resorting to sign language'

'Prove assistants understand me by getting what I intend to buy'

Action plan: Use 'Learn to speak French' audio tapes.

How do you test whether you have met the criteria for a goal? The measurements in that example are fairly easy to test. If our French speaker goes into a *boulangerie* and comes out with a *baguette* instead of a croissant, it will be obvious that the criteria have not been met and the goal has not been achieved. If, on the other hand, the French speaker uses no sign language, asks for a croissant and emerges with one, the goal will have been achieved.

In the early stages of starting to use the goal-setting process, it can be difficult to differentiate between the goal, the criteria and the action plans. It sometimes helps to think of the process as an athletics race in which:

• Goal = the finishing line for the event

• Criteria = individual hurdles that contestants must clear

• Action plans = the training necessary to clear the hurdles and reach the finishing line.

In the example we have just used, our French beginner has set a personal finishing line, the goal of speaking French. Because she realises that it would be possible to go into a shop in France and obtain what she wants by sign language, she has set two hurdles which she has to clear to reach her desired level of competence in French: using no sign language, and getting what she wants. Because she speaks no French at the moment, she has identified the training she will undertake before she attempts to clear the hurdles and reach the finishing line — her action plan is to use 'Learn to speak French' audio tapes. It is a very simple personal goal, with only two criteria and one action plan, and, because it is purely personal, she will assess for herself whether or not she meets the criteria and achieves the goal.

More complex goals, and goals which relate to professional competence, may have:

• Criteria which require verification by other people such as practice supervisors or tutors.

In a totally open learning system, all students are free to choose their own practice supervisor. They can approach a colleague they respect and who possesses any essential qualifications or experience for the role of practice supervisor in that particular setting. The colleague has, of course, to be willing to take on the responsibilities of practice supervision and to have managerial support.

Additionally, goals relating to the achievement of professional competences, and more complex personal goals, are likely to have:

- A number of criteria for measuring achievement

- Several action plans.

Let's look at the process again, this time setting a professional goal. Suppose you were undertaking a professional development course and were required to show evidence of good written communication with clients. You decide to produce an information leaflet on access to your department for people with physical disabilities. You might ask: 'Why not just go ahead without going through the goal-setting exercise?' The answer is that if you want to be sure you produce something worth offering clients you need to set criteria, and you may need some small areas of training to help you complete your task. You therefore need to set criteria and make action plans. Using the formal goal-setting process will also provide evidence of your achievement both for your own satisfaction and for your professional portfolio.

Because you have set this goal as part of professional development, your practice supervisor will be involved in agreeing the goal and the criteria for its achievement, and in assessing whether you have met the criteria.

The first draft of your goal might read:

Goal statement with timescale: Produce, in the next two months, an information leaflet describing the easiest route for ramp, lift and wheelchair access so that visitors with physical disabilities can reach us as easily as possible.

Criteria: Agreed with, and to be assessed by, my practice supervisor:

- No person with disabilities using the leaflet complains that there is an easier route.

Action plan: Survey the site.

Is this draft sufficient? The *goal statement* and *timescale* are adequate if it is possible to get the leaflet produced in that time. A brief run-through how long the site survey would take you, the time necessary to draft the leaflet and the time the print room would need to prepare the master copy and run off the number you require would soon check your timescale.

The criteria? How do you know that your leaflet is clear and easy to understand? Additionally, how do you really know that visitors who have disabilities are reaching you as easily as possible if you simply rely on complaints? Do you always complain if you are not satisfied or do you simply mutter under your breath and leave it at that? It would be better to rephrase and expand the criteria to read:

Criteria: Agreed with, and to be assessed by, my practice supervisor:

• All people with disabilities asked are satisfied with the layout and language of the leaflet and with the information it contains

• All people with disabilities asked are able to follow the directions easily

• No person with disabilities using the leaflet complains that there is an easier route.

If a visitor with disabilities complains that he/she cannot read or understand the leaflet or that there is a far simpler route than the one described in the leaflet, you will not have met your criteria.

The action plan? 'Survey the site' is certainly an essential part of the action required to produce the leaflet, but you might also consider 'researching suitable size, colour, typeface and terminology for leaflets for people who might have multiple disabilities, including visual impairment and learning difficulties'. Your action plans might then become:

Action plans:

• Survey the site for ramps, lifts and wheelchair access

• Research presentation for people with visual and other impairment

• Seek assistance from the learning difficulties unit on the use of terminology or symbols.

Courses and learning programmes which use goal-setting as part of personal and professional development and to assist in assessment of learning often provide students with printed sheets to simplify the process. On the sheets produced by the Emap Healthcare Open Learning Programme this goal would appear as shown on the record sheet on page 27. The record sheet for the action plan would appear as shown on page 28.

The goal-setting process ensures that you are clear about:

- What you are aiming to achieve

- When you intend to reach your goal

- Who will assess your achievement of a goal

- How success will be measured

- The action, or training, you need to undertake.

In a professional setting your tutor, or manager, will be able to follow your progress and assess your achievement. Where professional competence is concerned, the goal-setting process offers opportunities for you and your assessor to discuss and agree the criteria for successful achievement of goals.

Goal-setting is particularly helpful because it goes beyond an assessor making a judgement without having to state the criteria used to make that judgement. Equally, goal-setting allows measurement of the highest level of achievement each individual is capable of, which may be far beyond the level of criteria set by others divorced from the learning process. Finally, although goal-setting is individual to each student, the explicit statement of criteria for the achievement of goals means that comparison can be made with judgements made by other assessors of other students. Assessment of competence using the goal-setting process allows assessors to compare standards of competence in greater detail than most other methods and, in doing so, may offer greater reliability in assessment.

A word of advice. Be modest in your initial goal-setting. It is a good idea to get used to the goal-setting process by using it at first to achieve personal goals such as improving your study skills.

One example might be:

'Learn to use the college library effectively within six weeks so that I can find relevant books and research reports.'

Goal Plan Record Sheet

| Example | Date: 28/10/96 |

Name: *Jane Smith*

Place of work: *Birchfield General*

Details of those responsible for tutoring/supervising/managing your professional development:

Name: *Ms A. Macintosh*   Status: *Manager*

Goal statement with timescale

Produce, in the next two months, an information leaflet describing the easiest route for ramp, lift and wheelchair access.

Criteria for success

Agreed with, and to be assessed by, my practice supervisor:

1. *All people with disabilities asked are satisfied with the layout and language of the leaflet and with the information it contains*

2. *All people with disabilities asked are able to follow the directions easily*

3. *No person with disabilities using the leaflet complains that there is an easier route.*

Summary statements: Revised goal plans?

Your statement:

                              Signature: Date:

- -

Statement of person supporting/supervising your development?

Name: *Ann Macintosh*   Status: *Manager*   Signature: Date:

Action Plan Record Sheet

| Example | Date: 28/10/96 |

Name: *Jane Smith*

Place of work: *Birchfield General*

Identity No.: *NT123450*
(if available)

Person supporting/supervising your development
Name: *Ann Macintosh*   Status: *Manager*

Action plan (How will you go about achieving the goal?)

Deadline: 28/12/96
Review date

* *Survey the site for ramps, lifts and wheelchair access*

* *Research presentation for people with visual and other impairment*

* *Seek assistance from the learning difficulties unit on the use of terminology or symbols*

Support/resources needed

Review statements:

Date:

Your review statement:

Signature: Date:

Review statement of person responsible for supporting/supervising your development?

Name: *Ann Macintosh*   Status: *Manager*   Signature: Date:

The fully stated goal would be:

Goal statement with timescale: Learn to use the college library effectively within six weeks.

Criteria: Agreed with, and to be assessed by, my tutor:

- I can obtain books and research reports I require from our library, finding them for myself

- I can obtain books and research reports from other sources, through our library.

Action plans:

- Attend new-term library users' introductory session

- Spend half an hour every evening after work in the he library until I can find my way around it

- Practice using the index systems to find books and reports I already know about on the shelves

- Ask the librarian to set me some 'tests' to find books and research reports I have not seen before, stocked by our library

- Ask the librarian to teach me how to obtain items from other sources, if this is not covered in the introductory session.

If you find setting criteria difficult to begin with, it can sometimes help to think of some people who have the ability you hope to achieve. Ask yourself what you can see or otherwise measure in them or their performance that enables you to say: 'I can be sure that they have that knowledge/skill/ appropriate attitude because...'. The way in which you measure their knowledge/skill/attitude can be transferred to become the criteria for your own goal to achieve them.

Here is an example. Suppose you have just transferred to a new work area in which peer assessment is used as a major element in quality control. At your first group discussion you are struck both by your own difficulty in contributing positively and by the successful way another member of the group does so. Later, two other colleagues comment on how well that same group member undertakes the process of peer assessment, and between the three of you, you identify exactly what it is that she does that makes her contributions so effective. You agree that this person is always objective, cites specific instances without unduly criticising any particular individual, adopts a non-threatening body posture and verbal approach and offers positive feedback and suggestions for improving group performance.

You decide to set a professional development goal using those identified actions as observable and measurable criteria. Additionally, you decide to ask your colleagues, as well as your practice supervisor, to play a part in assessing your performance because you feel that this may contribute to group learning as well as to your own development.

Your goal reads:

Goal: Contribute positively and effectively in peer group quality-control meetings.

Criteria: Agreed with, and to be assessed by, my practice supervisor and my peers, I must:

• Use non-threatening verbal and non-verbal communication

• Be objective in my comments, not swayed by personal likes or dislikes

• Support comments with specific evidence

• Comment without implying censure of individual colleagues

• Offer positive feedback

• Offer positive suggestions for improvement of group performance.

Action plans:

• Carry out a small literature search and read up on group dynamics and on peer assessment

• Revise my knowledge and understanding of peer assessment in quality assurance

• Discuss with my successful colleague the way in which she prepares for a meeting

- Ask her if she will allow me to observe her, particularly over the next few meetings, and if she will discuss her contribution afterwards with me

- Add to my list any further criteria which become apparent, with the agreement of my practice supervisor and my colleagues.

You then have a set of criteria which are themselves subject to peer assessment and a workable set of action plans to meet them. A great additional advantage of setting criteria of this sort is that the involvement of colleagues in the process causes all people concerned to discuss and justify their own standards and to arrive at a consensus on measurable criteria for knowledge, skills and attitudes in any set of circumstances. That can only help to improve professional standards.

Always set relatively small goals with shortish timescales, and aim to have only two to four in hand at any one time. Misguided souls have sometimes set themselves the goal of taking over the world by Wednesday week, but they have usually come to grief, wasting a great deal of time and effort and causing themselves a lot of distress in the process.

Because profiling is a continuing process which helps to chart your progress and to reassess your strengths and areas for development, you need a means of logging that progress. Keeping a professional diary helps you to do this and we shall start our next chapter by looking at the diary-keeping process.

3: Study skills

IN THIS CHAPTER WE SHALL:

- **Consider ways of organising your study time**
- **Discuss how to make the best use of study materials**
- **Discuss tutorial support**
- **Consider how you and your fellow students can help each other**

Once you have decided to become an opening learning student you have taken on responsibility for your own learning. This means that as well as gaining the freedom to study as you wish, you also take responsibility for:

- Managing your own study schedule

- Using study materials

- Contributing to any group sessions you attend.

We will consider each of these in turn.

Finding the time to study

Fitting studying into an already busy life needs careful planning. It might help to have a piece of paper beside you as we go through this section, so that you can jot down items you want to take into account when planning your own study schedule.

For most of us, finding the time to study is the biggest problem in becoming an open learning student. Once we find the solution we are already halfway to success. In fact, planning study time is so crucial that you may want to make it one of your first goals.

How much time?

The first question to ask is: 'How much study time will I need?' Many distance learning courses suggest average study times, either for units of study or for individual exercises within them. Many people find such guidelines helpful, but they can cause others to panic, either because the particular piece of study takes them far longer than the recommended time or, sometimes, because it takes them far less.

In the first instance you may be left feeling that you really can't be very bright. In the latter case you may go through the material again and again because you are convinced that, to take as long as it says, there must be more in it than you have understood. Both situations can leave you feeling very unsure of yourself. If this happens to you it may help to remember that 'average times' are just that. In the long run you are likely to find that sometimes you will take longer and sometimes less than the time indicated. That is one of the great strengths of open learning — you can use whatever length of time suits you. However, when you begin your initial planning, any 'average times' can be a helpful starting point.

Next, you need to identify time within your normal schedule when you can reasonably expect to be able to study. It might be a good idea at this stage to sit down and work out exactly how you spend your time at the moment. Look at it this way. If you spend eight hours in 24 sleeping, eight hours working and two hours eating, washing and so on, you still have six hours left. Of course there are still major tasks which can fill those six hours, such as looking after children, the garden, the housework and similar chores, but do they — need they — take all that time?

Make detailed notes of exactly how you spent your time in the past seven days and mark all the items that are essential, such as work and meal times. Then highlight any activities that are not essential, for example reading newspapers, and any time which passed without being 'used' at all. If you find that you have spent time on non-essential activities, perhaps cutting the grass twice in a week, or idly watching television, or even gazing into space putting off doing something like the ironing, then you do have some spare usable time.

You now need to think about organising your essential activities so that you can give yourself periods of time for study. Your personal study style will be very important in making this decision. Some people like to study in long sessions of several hours, while others prefer a series of shorter periods. Profiling will have helped you to identify the way in which you like to study, so bear this in mind when planning your study time. The basic study plan of one independent learner is shown overleaf.

Study time: Average student on this open learning course needs eight hours a week.

Like to study in sessions of no less than two hours and find I concentrate better in the evenings. Will do:

- **Four hours in the evening of my second day-off each week, plus**
- **Two hours two evenings a week.**

Using study materials

Setting up your 'study'

The next thing you need to do once you have 'found' time to study is to decide where you are going to study. The ideal situation is to have a room, a 'study', in fact, or even just a table where you can set out your materials and leave them ready to pick up again at any time. Unfortunately, few of us have that sort of luxury, and have to do the best we can in the kitchen or anywhere else where we can escape with our study materials.

In such circumstances it helps to have a large box into which you can 'file' your course materials. A ring-binder file to hold your notes and some sort of case for pens and highlighters will complete your basic student's equipment, and the box then becomes your 'study'.

Organising your study sequence

Although you will have begun to organise your commitments so that you have time to study, you will need to take the process further by organising the sequence in which you will study the course components. Many open learning courses have a variety of materials and part of the art of becoming an independent learner lies in organising the way you work through them. Some open learning courses provide students with a study plan, showing the order in which materials should be studied. Here is the beginning of a plan for a course which uses a variety of materials and media, the 'units' being specially written text:

COURSE PLAN

Week 1: Unit 1 Part 1: Chapters 1 & 2 Course Reader.

Week 2: Unit 1 Part 2: Tape 1 Side A
Anything from the Unit 1 items on the 'Further reading list'.

Week 3: Unit 1 Part 3: Chapters 5 & 9 Course Reader.

Week 4: Unit 1 Part 4: Video 1
Submit first written assignment for assessment

The course plan continues in this way for the entire year, including revision time and the date of the formal examination. If your course does not provide you with such a plan, you may find the completely open schedule difficult to come to terms with at first. One way of coping is to organise your own study sequence and draw up your own schedule.

If, for example, you receive a whole year's study materials consisting of three 10-week core units and two supplementary six-week modules, you can plan your 'study year' for yourself. Draw a rough sheet showing the 52 weeks of the year and mark holidays and breaks such as Christmas when you will not do much studying. Then decide on the order in which you want to study the core units and the supplementary modules. Pencil these in on your year plan, allocating to each unit or module the numbers of weeks you think it is likely to take. The course information should help you with this task, but sometimes you just have to look at the overall number of weeks available and fit the study schedule into them.

The more open the timescale of the course, the more flexible this process can be. If there is no constraint on how long it takes you to complete the course, you can allocate as many weeks to each component as you want. If there are deadlines imposed on you, such as submission dates for assessed work or examinations, you will have to organise your study schedule to meet them. If you do have to meet such deadlines, you may find it helpful to aim for completion dates some days in advance of the deadlines. This means that you will have time in hand in case you get flu, or a sudden crisis at work forces you to do overtime. Put these earlier completion dates on your study plan as well as the actual submission dates.

Once you have the basic schedule, with deadlines pencilled in, you can look at the requirements for study of each component. You can then fill in the fine detail, such as which part of which unit you will study in each week, and what supplementary material, such as course books or further reading, you will also use that week. If the course involves gaining particular practical experience, you will need to note where this is likely to occur and to plan ahead by gaining managerial support and the co-operation of colleagues. We will discuss these vital factors shortly.

Try not to become too worried initially about the sequence in which you study different elements. Open learning courses are often designed so that smaller units stand alone. Fully open courses are designed to allow students the freedom of working their way through components in any order. While it is likely that in a less open course you will gain most from studying materials in a particular sequence, you can always recap on material you have read 'too early' or catch up on any that you have somehow wrongly scheduled. That is one of the great benefits of open learning.

Do also remember that 'additional reading' lists are just that. Students are rarely expected to read everything on the list but you should try to read a representative sample. If, for any reason, you cannot obtain something from a further reading list, use your library skills, or obtain the advice of your tutor or librarian in finding a comparable work.

Overall, the advice here is: 'Don't panic'. Once you get under way as an open learner you will rapidly become skilled at sequencing materials and at juggling study time.

Getting the most from materials

Once you have found yourself a place to study and sorted out the sequence in which you will use the materials, you need to try out various ways of gaining the most from them. Some people like to read through a complete piece of study material, listen to tapes and watch any videos for that part of the course without initially making any notes. Having gained an overview of that part of the study, they then repeat the process, noting down important points and their own arguments and views as they do so.

Other people like to work slowly through each piece of text, tape or video, making notes as they go along. They feel that this enables them to concentrate on each section more easily than if they already knew what was to follow. After the initial detailed read they may cover the materials a second time more rapidly to ensure that they have a balanced overview.

Whether the arguments are being presented in text, on tape, on screen or face-to-face, you always need to think about them critically, by asking:

- Who are the people presenting the knowledge, ideas or arguments? Are they credible?

- Are their claims to knowledge supported by sound academic references?

- Are their arguments logical, rational and unbiased?

Strings of qualifications and years of experience do not necessarily mean that an individual puts forward credible information or arguments, and you should always carry out this sort of critique as you study.

One great advantage of using study materials rather than face-to-face teaching is that you can re-run the 'lecture' in text or on tape as often as you need until you are sure you understand and have got everything from it that you want. Additionally, you can use the materials in whatever way, or order, suits you best. How you study really depends on the way your mind works. Once again, profiling will have helped you identify that vital aspect of being an independent student.

Making useful notes

Why make notes? Note-making helps you to identify the most important facts, opinions or arguments being presented and to be able to run through them rapidly later. Although it would be nice to be able to remember every word — and some people can — most of us are not so lucky. If we can't remember everything, we need a way of selecting the vital points.

How do you decide what is vital? It's a bit like life. Each day is full of happenings, many of them interesting, but only a few of them are essential for survival or necessary for future reference. Study materials are just the same, but they usually have one advantage — the people who prepared them have already organised them under headings for you.

These headings highlight the fact that there is an important piece of information or argument in the material that follows. Any notes you make are likely to use the headings to signpost the areas covered. Each heading is likely to have two or three lines summarising the information or arguments in the text. It is useful to include the number of the page from which the note was made, such as 'Unit 4, Management techniques, Page 43', so that you can easily refer back to the original in the future if you need to do so.

With tapes or videos it often helps to use the 'pause' button while you note down points you want to remember. Making notes from 'alive' speakers is more difficult, and tape-recording them and making notes later is often helpful. Notes that are so detailed that they are nearly as long as the course materials are a waste of time. Remember that the whole point of note-making is to identify and record the essential facts or arguments.

Some people prefer to use a highlighter pen on text rather than actually writing notes. This certainly saves time initially but can be a problem if you want to use the 'notes' later where there is limited space. Fellow passengers on buses and trains may tolerate you studying from a folder with notes but may be less happy when you unload three carrier bags full of course materials. This method may also cost you more time revising because you will have to go through every bit of material again to find the highlighted portions.

Sometimes it helps to record your notes onto an audio tape so that you can play them back when using public transport. In this way you can muse further on ideas and arguments you have read or watched on video or can help commit facts to memory. Alternatively, you might like to condense vital points onto postcard-size 'flash cards', which can be carried in your pocket or briefcase and referred to at intervals. Again, these can stimulate your thought processes and help commit vital facts to memory. Making flash cards at the same time as you read main notes will provide an early foundation in preparing for revision before examinations, and reinforces the learning process.

In note-taking, as in other aspects of study, you need to decide what works best for you. The notes are yours, so make them in whatever way will be of most help to you.

Using libraries effectively

Although you may be provided with the basic materials for your course, you will almost always be required, and want, to pursue your studies more broadly. You will want to read more widely and may need to follow up references or develop particular lines of inquiry. Libraries are study 'mines' where you can search for, and find, virtually any information you require. It makes sense, therefore, to become skilled in using libraries as soon as possible.

It is easy to be intimidated by libraries when you go in for the first time. The silence in an academic library can be awe-inspiring and everyone in there seems to know exactly what they are about. You should not, however, be intimidated.

The first thing to do is to obtain information on how a particular library 'works'. Even if you understand the basic systems by which most libraries are organised, you may still have problems when you change libraries. One large university always offers its higher-degree students a session with a librarian. Very few of these students turn up to the session, believing that they already know how to use any library. They may, of course, but they may also need to have the idiosyncrasies of that particular library explained. As a result of their overconfidence, they are often found in the following weeks asking other people if they know where to find particular items. The moral of the story is that no one should expect to be immediately at home in a strange library.

All libraries have the books on their shelves listed in 'catalogues' or 'indexes', usually under the headings of 'Subject', 'Author' and 'Title'. The indexes may be on cards, filed in alphabetical order, or on computer screen or microfiche. To search the subject indexes you need to identify 'Key' words under which useful items might be classified. If you want a book on historical research skills, your first key words will be 'Research methods', but you might also try 'History', 'Archives' or 'Census'.

Although most libraries are organised in similar ways, the allocation of items to classifications in catalogues and indexes can vary and you may need to use your imagination in trying different key words. Be persistent if you want to track down as many items on your subject as possible. Computerised catalogues make subject searches relatively easy, as you can search using a variety of key words fairly rapidly.

Author indexes are simpler. If you know that someone called 'Floud' has written a book on historical research methods but you can't remember the title, you will look in the author index for the name 'Floud'.

If you know the title but you can't remember the author you will look in the title index under 'An introduction to quantitative methods for historians'.

The microfiche or computer terminals in different libraries are not necessarily the same, so you should never feel that you ought to know how they work in an unfamiliar library. If you are ever in any doubt, ask one of the librarians. They work in libraries because they want people to use the library facilities. They are there to help you.

Books are grouped on library shelves according to their 'classification', such as 'Nursing' or 'Dermatology'. The index will tell you what classification each book is in, and a plan of the library showing which shelves each classification is on will then allow you to find the actual book.

Magazines and journals are a valuable and up-to-date source of research findings, ideas and information. One of the differences between school-age and adult education is that children are often discouraged from reading magazines, except as a way to promote reading skills, and are encouraged instead to read only books. Adults soon learn that academic journals provide essential access to current debate. Research findings, ideas and arguments are reported and aired in academic and professional journals long before they appear in books and all adult learners should make use of a wide range of such publications. Libraries usually display a complete list of the journals which they take. Recent issues are usually prominently displayed and back issues are filed under the journal title, all titles being ranked alphabetically.

Most professional journals produce a contents index which should be filed with each year's issues. If you cannot find the index for a year's issues, ask the librarian for assistance, as the index may be filed for safe keeping. Some journals publish abstracts of articles, summarising their contents. These are a great help in deciding whether it is worth reading the whole article or not.

If you need to carry out an in-depth search, it may be possible for your librarian to help you undertake an 'on-line' search. This enables you to search computerised records of items relating to your particular interest which are held in other locations. On-line searching takes time and can be very expensive, so it is wise to take the advice of your librarian when deciding whether to use such facilities or not.

If you need a book or a copy of an article that is not held in your library, the librarian will usually be able to get it for you through an inter-library loan. A fee may be charged, so it is wise to check before requesting this service. Libraries are usually happy to allow non-members reference facilities if you simply want to read through books or articles in their collection.

Finally, students are sometimes advised against simply searching along shelves for useful volumes. While it is always essential to undertake a full index and/or on-line search when undertaking a literature search, it can be helpful to augment this by 'shelf crawling'. Although you will search subject and title indexes using key words, there may be other volumes with individual chapters relating to your topic which a formal search may not find. A slow prowl along shelves of related classifications, looking down the contents lists of each book can prove rewarding.

Making best use of your tutor

In Chapter 1 we described the equal partnership that open learners have with their tutors. Some students find this difficult at first because their previous experience has been that teachers are in charge and are there to 'teach'. These students may therefore go along to their first tutorial expecting the tutor to stand in front of a blackboard and tell them all they should know. Open learning is not like that! For a start, where open learning is combined with the distance method, you already have 'tutors-in-text'. These are the people who have prepared the study materials by writing the texts and the scripts or scenarios for audio and video-tapes. In effect, you already have a cupboard full of tutors. Using face-to-face tutorial time to go over ground already covered in the materials is a waste of time.

Because open learning tries to remove barriers to learning, open learning courses can result in incredible intellectual growth for students. The tutor is there to stimulate students to think, to appraise a variety of viewpoints critically and to put forward new ideas which they can support with rational arguments. You will find that open learning tutors use a wide variety of methods, such as group discussions, student-led debates and role play, to encourage you to develop these intellectual skills. The actual study level of the course has little to do with whether it is a degree, vocational or recreational course, because the process of opening minds is common to all.

Many students like to have some reassurance that they have identified the 'vital' pieces of information or arguments in the course materials. Your tutor may therefore devise some way of providing that feedback, at the same time taking you a step further in your development or in the arguments started in the materials. For example, if the study materials have discussed time management, the tutor may offer the group an exercise which takes your experience or understanding of the subject further. In doing this you will all have the opportunity to test whether you have understood, and can apply, the theories explained in the study materials. You are then likely to go home feeling that your independent study was fruitful and that the time spent at the tutorial was worth the effort of getting there.

In that last paragraph we described the tutor as 'offering' the group an exercise. Because open learning is about choice, the place, time and content of a tutorial is often negotiated between each tutor and the student group. This is a very delicate process, and is most successful when the group promotes one another's learning. We will return to this shortly when we discuss group support.

Other routes of communication between tutors and students

Written communication: If you submit written work your tutor will return it to you with written comments. You should not view this with alarm, because the written comments replace the verbal comments that would have been made in the classroom in a conventional face-to-face course.

It is important to remember that your tutor is there to help you. Many people returning to study after a break have initial problems with their written work, especially essays and in-depth projects. Do ask your tutor to expand on comments or to give you additional advice on improving your written work if you feel this would be helpful. Open learning tutors are very sympathetic to these types of problems and are skilled at helping students overcome them.

Telephone communication: If you need to telephone your tutor, check the information you have been given to see if there is a request to use a particular time. Tutors often have full-time occupations in addition to supporting open learning students and they also have a home life. Try to respect their other commitments and use their time wisely. Always be quite clear before you telephone, exactly how you hope they will be able to help you and be prepared to ring again if you hit an inconvenient time. A tutor telephoned in the middle of bathing the baby might not be best placed to carry on an in-depth discussion on analysing research documents. Before telephoning your tutor you should:

- Be clear in your own mind exactly how you hope the tutor can help you

- Have the unit/module/page number ready to quote if necessary

- Re-read the part that is causing you problems to ensure that it is not simply a reading error (such things can happen!)

- Be prepared to explain your problem and call the tutor back later when he/she has had time to refer to the course materials or clarify his/her own thoughts.

Individual tutorials: These may be used for confidential discussions, for example on assessment or where a student is experiencing particular difficulties.

Group support

If you attend tutorials you may find yourself part of a very varied group. Because this is open learning you will have the opportunity to learn from your fellow students and they, in their turn, may learn from you. It often takes a few meetings for a group to settle down together and the process can be helped if all students try to be aware of:

* The need for each group member to contribute (if no one says anything there will be no group discussion)

* The need to avoid hogging the limelight, always jumping in first with an opinion

* The values, beliefs and opinions of others, however much they might disagree with them

* The uncertainty and lack of confidence that is not far from the surface in most of us.

We can all help one another in these situations if we have respect for the unique mix of knowledge, skills and attitudes that each of us brings with us. We can then concentrate on study without unnecessarily distracting each other.

Student networking

Many groups form support networks in which the members exchange telephone numbers or arrange group meetings in addition to tutorials. The advantages are that this:

* Allows you to explore the subject as a group more fully than tutorial time allows

* Provides peer support from others who understand what you are studying and the method by which you are studying

* Allows many extra ideas and perspectives to be contributed to the learning process.

Possible disadvantages are that

* An articulate individual may misinterpret information or arguments in the

materials and convince the group that he/she is right. Without the tutor being present the whole group may be led up a 'blind alley'

- Your own development and learning may be held back by the needs or opinions of the group.

As with tutorials, there is no right or wrong. It is up to each individual to decide whether he or she finds taking part in peer support groups helpful or not.

Managing your family and friends

The people who love us can be our worst enemies! They like to be with us and, because we also love them, we like to do things for them. For an independent student studying at home, gaining the co-operation of family and friends is vital. It is a good idea to sit down with those who have been used to being the centre of your attention and talk through this new notion of you as a student. Many people find that their nearest and dearest are very supportive, but it may take time and some assertiveness on your part before this comes about.

Veronica was in her 40s and working part time when she became an open learning student. Her husband and three children all led busy lives. Although they all said that they thought it a good idea for Veronica to study and that they would give her a hand with her housework, they initially didn't do very much. When their shirts were not ironed, or the supper was late, they made their displeasure obvious, albeit by joking.

It took Veronica a great deal of belief in her own right to study before she pointed out that the ironing that wanted doing and the stomachs waiting to be filled were their responsibility, not hers. The housework was not hers. With her job and her study she now worked as many hours a week as they did. After a stunned silence everyone in the household agreed to a fairer distribution of chores.

You may also have to spell out to family and friends your need to study without interruption. It is no help at all when, deep in a mental debate that is stretching your brain to bursting point, the door opens and a voice says: 'I say, Mum, what does "annihilate" mean?' Pointing out that you are strongly tempted to try some hands-on practice rather than explaining the word may help assure an interruption-free future.

Gaining support from managers and colleagues

Your managers may have played a very positive part in encouraging you to study, perhaps by allocating you funding and study time. If so, they are likely to continue this support by discussing your studies with you and helping you to explore new study-related ideas. If your managers have not initially been involved in this way, and your studies do relate to your work, you should try to gain their co-operation and that of other colleagues early in your course. Their support will be of great practical benefit, and their ideas may not only enrich your learning but also have positive benefits for your work environment. Where a course requires that you gain experience in, or obtain information from, other work areas, the co-operation of your own managers, and of the managers of those areas, is essential.

Negotiating access to other areas

However open a course, and however much responsibility you take for negotiating and arranging visits or work practice exchanges, you will obviously have to tread carefully. Where a number of students require similar work experience, it may be helpful if managers in different work areas make initial arrangements between themselves, leaving individual students to complete the fine details. Make sure that all concerned have adequate information on the course you are studying, its academic or professional status in relation to your work, and your work-related study needs.

You will need to approach this with considerable insight into the problems of busy managers. Few managers, who are already probably at full stretch, will feel kindly disposed to a voice on the telephone asking to 'Come along this afternoon to talk to your staff and see how your unit works' or to 'Swap with one of your staff for a fortnight starting next Monday'. If you need to gain this sort of experience as part of your course it is sensible to:

- Discuss your work experience/fact-finding needs with your own manager

- Make your first approach in writing to managers of other areas stating clearly why experience/information from their area is important to your studies

- Suggest ways in which this might be achieved without inconveniencing them and their workforce

- Suggest ways in which your visit might benefit their work area such as arranging an exchange visit with your place of work, or by providing feedback on other similar visits in a summary of any report you may be writing as part of your course

- Ensure that you have either a letter of introduction from your manager or tutor, or some form of identification, when making study-related visits.

In open learning, students may be linked to colleges a long way from home, which may mean negotiating library and other academic access in your own area. If you are in this situation you will need to find out what facilities are available and to negotiate access to them. Again, managerial and tutorial support is invaluable. In some instances you may be asked to pay for these facilities, so early inquiries will help you plan your study budget.

Gaining the co-operation of colleagues

In most groups there is some sort of hierarchy, whether it is formal or informal. Wherever you are in that hierarchy the fact that you are undertaking a course of study may alter people's perceptions of you and subtly affect the dynamics of the group. Colleagues may react in a number of ways, some supportive, some less so.

Jane, whose difficulties in getting to tutorials we described in Chapter 1, initially also had problems with her colleagues at work when they found out that she was studying. None of them had ever studied unless forced to do so. When Jane took her course material to work with her to read in her lunch break, one of the group picked up her notes and read them out.

'Management styles? What are they? What a load of jargon!'

By the time their lunch break was over the whole group knew a little more about management styles and Jane had had valuable practice at presenting ideas to and debating ideas with a sceptical audience. An even greater 'plus' was that one member of the group had become genuinely interested and proved an ongoing source of support. When Jane needed time off for a study workshop, this colleague readily offered to stand in so that Jane could be released.

Where studies relate to professional practice, colleagues may feel threatened. They may be acutely aware that they are not abreast of current debates related to practice and may fear that your new knowledge and insights may expose their own inadequacies. Sharing study materials and activities with colleagues and involving them in debate can prove a very positive way of overcoming such fears, helping them to learn and strengthening and increasing your own learning in the process.

Appraising your open learning study skills

Drawing all these threads together, we can see that there are a number of specific study skills which play a vital part in the lives of open learning students (see Fig 1). These skills obviously overlap, and will differ in their degree of importance from student to student, course to course and at different times.

Fig. 1. Open learning study skills

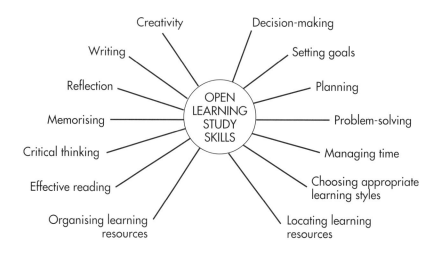

If you decide that open learning is for you, one of your first tasks will be to assess which of these skills you need to improve to help with your learning. Your personal profile will assist this process and your tutor is likely to be able to offer additional skills assessment and advice.

In the next chapter we shall consider ways in which you can monitor your progress as an open learning student, another process in which your colleagues can be involved.

4: Charting progress

IN THIS CHAPTER WE SHALL:

- **Discuss critical-incident analysis**
- **Consider what it means to use reflection in practice**
- **Describe ways in which you can use a diary to chart progress**

Charting a different course

In Chapter 1 we said that open learning was like having an open mind. Indeed, having an open mind is one of the basic requirements of being an open learner, because open learning students approach their studies as a quest for understanding and growth.

If you think back to the person you were five years ago, you are likely to be able to see some changes in yourself. The most obvious changes may be in your waistline or your hairstyle, but they are only surface changes. What about you as a person? Have you changed at a deeper level?

Most of us change continually, as we are exposed to different experiences. Often we may undergo profound changes in our attitudes and our abilities to cope but be almost unaware that this is happening, particularly in the middle of a busy life. If we don't reflect on these experiences we may waste much that we could have learnt from them, and restrict the development of new abilities and strengths.

> Pam hated having to return faulty items to shops, finding it easier to blame herself for poor purchases. One day she got home having bought an expensive blouse only to find that there was a fault in the weave of the material on the front of it. There was no way that she could wear the blouse and, because it had cost so much, she knew that she would have to try to get it exchanged. The shop staff were initially unhelpful, saying that she should have noticed the fault before she bought the blouse.
>
> Spurred on by the thought of the money she would have wasted if the blouse was not exchanged, Pam persisted. Eventually, because they had not got another blouse like it, the shop staff refunded Pam's money.
>
> At the time it was a major victory for Pam, but the next time she found that a cheaper item was not what she expected, she reverted to her previous ways. She made the fact that it had not cost much an excuse for not taking it back.

When we are at work we can also have experiences which might help us to develop new skills if only we see them as constructive learning experiences.

> Misha was a team leader who had completed his first line-management course. He generally got on well with people and enjoyed working with his colleagues. Unfortunately his unit suffered an outbreak of food poisoning and Misha undertook to tighten up on general hygiene.
>
> Seeing a member of staff in the kitchen rinsing a cup she had just used under the tap and then putting it back on the shelf ready for someone else to use, Misha, without thinking, said: 'Come on, Debbie, that's not good enough. All cups should be washed up properly.' Debbie retorted that she had washed the cup up properly and, before he realised what was happening, Misha found that he was in the middle of a real argument, which was being listened to by other members of staff.
>
> Debbie lodged a formal complaint against Misha. They were both disciplined, Debbie for breaching health and safety rules and Misha for not behaving in the way expected of a manager. Misha felt aggrieved and simply put the experience out of his mind as something painful he preferred not to think about.

When it comes to academic work, many of us prefer to remember high marks and forget the less successful outcomes. While this is only human, the truth of the matter is that if we took greater note of the areas where we did less well we would have a better chance of doing well all round.

> Doug was a mature student who had considered himself to be already fairly well educated when he decided to study for a degree. His first piece of assessed work just scraped a pass mark, and the tutor had written a lot of comments aimed at helping Doug improve his performance in future assignments. The first comment described his style of writing as being 'journalistic'. Since he had passed the assignment Doug did not take a great deal of notice and was outraged when his second assignment was failed, with the same comment prominent on it. Doug rang up the department and demanded his money back, saying that the tutor who had marked his work, 'that lad in jeans', obviously didn't know what he was talking about.

Critical-incident analysis

Any incident which offers an opportunity to look at ourselves, our lives, and the way we work or study can be described as a 'critical incident'. All three people whose experiences we have just described could have used those episodes far more constructively if they had reflected on what was happening, both as it happened and after the event. Such incidents can be critical to our learning and self-development. We should therefore resist the temptation to plough on regardless in the middle of an incident or to put it immediately out of our minds when it is over. Instead, we should try to analyse what is happening or has happened, so that we can learn from it and put our learning to good use. The same argument applies to successful incidents. We should analyse what made them successful, so that we can use those strategies again in the future.

Charles Handy[8], who specialises in helping people develop management skills, uses the following argument for self-development:

'At school I knew one thing for sure, that every problem in the world had already been solved by someone. The answers to many of them were in the teacher's head or in the back of their textbook. If they were not, then they were bound to be in someone else's head or in someone else's book. The message I carried along with me was clear. If you meet with an unfamiliar problem, find the expert, usually someone older or more senior than yourself, and ask.

'It was a crippling message. Until I unlearnt it, at about the age of 35, I was a meek underling, obedient, on the whole, but dull, unaware of my own capabilities and sometimes doubting whether I had any. I had "learnt", or thought I had, that people in higher jobs than me inevitably knew more than me and inevitably were right. I had acquired for myself the assumption of stupidity — my stupidity — when what I really needed was the habit of curiosity.'

To move forward towards growth as individuals we need to let go of the security of the person we think we are, and continually question ourselves, our surroundings and the societies and organisations in which we live and work. In doing so we should expect to find our own answers to problems. Critical-incident analysis is central to that process.

Imagine for a minute that you are part of a team in a client-centred profession. You are working in a unit that is short of virtually everything except clients: short of staff, short of funds and short of temper.

You walk into a room to find two colleagues having a real humdinger of an argument about the time one of them has spent with one client. You apologise for interrupting, saying that you will leave them to it but if an independent adjudicator would help. . . ?

Cont...

...cont

Your colleagues accept your offer, put their argument before you and enter into a more civilised discussion which resolves their difficulties.

Afterwards you sit down and analyse what it was you did that helped bring this about. You conclude that by pure chance you:

- **Recognised a potentially team-damaging situation**

- **Made time to help**

- **Defused the tense atmosphere**

- **Presented yourself as a neutral arbitrator who facilitated resolution of the conflict.**

You conclude that these were effective strategies and decide to employ them in similar situations in the future.

Critical-incident analysis is a constructive way of learning from real life. It can be applied to the ways in which we have dealt with acute practical situations, with interpersonal relationships, with intellectual skills, with anything that has revealed strengths or weaknesses in our performance or the performance of others. The crux of critical-incident analysis is that it is a way of identifying strengths and weaknesses, so that we can reinforce the former and overcome the latter.

Ethical and legal considerations

Because critical-incident analysis may have ethical and legal implications, you should always consider these aspects carefully before sharing your thoughts. While you may quite reasonably wish to avail yourself of the experience and skills of your tutor, manager or other colleagues in analysing any critical incident, there may be problems of confidentiality or ethical or legal constraints. If you think this may apply in any situation, you should consider very carefully what you can reveal. Although such restrictions may limit group discussion, critical-incident analysis can still be used in the broader field of reflective practice.

Reflective practice

Donald Schön[9], in his work on reflective practice, writes convincingly of the way in which we can all develop an open approach to new situations and experiences. Although his work is directed towards professional practitioners, it is relevant to all aspects of life. Schön believes that we should reflect on what we are doing while we are in the middle of action, and also afterwards, at our leisure. Such reflection can have far-reaching consequences for personal growth:

'As the professional moves towards new competences, he gives up some familiar sources of satisfaction and opens himself to new ones. He gives up the rewards of unquestioned authority, the freedom to practise without challenge to his competence, the comfort of relative invulnerability, the gratifications of deference. The new satisfactions open to him are largely about his knowledge-in-practice, and about himself. When a practitioner becomes a researcher into his own practice, he engages in a continuing process of self-education.'

When we carry out critical analysis of an incident as it happens we analyse:

• What is happening

• What has brought it about

• What is going well and what is not

• How the situation might be improved.

If Misha had carried out this sort of analysis when he first saw Debbie rinsing the cup, he would not have made the errors he did in correcting her in the hearing of others. When we carry out critical-incident analysis after an event we can take a more leisurely approach, asking

• What happened

• What brought it about

• What in the incident went well

• What did not go well

• What alternative action might have been taken to improve the situation

• What can we learn from the incident to influence our action in future?

Misha could reflect that in future he would pause and think before saying the first thing that came into his head, a sequence known as 'engage brain before opening mouth'. Second, he would never again correct staff in the hearing of others. Finally he would realise that he had progressed as a manager from the analysis of this painful incident, and decide that in future he would routinely analyse any critical incident and learn from it in a similar way.

One way of encouraging reflective practice, both in our personal lives and in our professional practice, in whatever field we work, is by keeping a reflective diary.

A reflective diary

Most of us have had experience of a variety of types of diary. At home we probably have a diary that logs gripping reminders such as 'the plumber is coming on Wednesday' or that we have to 'go to the dentist on Friday'. Some of us keep personal diaries in which we write private thoughts and hopes. Work diaries usually record meetings and appointments with colleagues and clients and form a vital part of our lives in organising our work schedules.

A reflective diary is rather different. Here are some excerpts from diaries kept by Jenny, an open learning student. They relate to her personal characteristics, her job and her studies. You will see that later in the diary she has returned to earlier entries and reflected on what she has learnt:

29/11 This is my first entry. I have decided to keep a diary to assess my progress as the course goes along. I have completed the profile pack and, looking back to it, it has made me look at myself closely; that is, values and beliefs, strengths and weaknesses, what I have achieved and what I want to achieve. There is so much to learn; this course has given me the buzz and I am raring to go.

10/12 I am trying to set a goal and finding it hard: unable to write a direct goal and state reasonable criteria. The example given looks so easy but I cannot crack it. Will see David (tutor).

8/5 Goal-setting is really flowing now. Looking back to my earlier problem, it is worth all the effort I had to put in and all the help David gave me. I measure all my achievements objectively now.

4/7 I am so much more aware and questioning of my own actions than I used to be. I had a good rapport with clients in the past, but looking back my input was inadequate. I am more knowledgeable and more up to date, especially in research. David says he has noticed this, too. But there is still so much to learn.

Sue, who works in a private hospital, used her diary to analyse a critical incident:

> 12/5 I was trying to jump the final hurdle today of management — being in charge on operations day. I began by making a wrong decision about work priorities and the operation list got slightly delayed, but my manager kindly sorted this out and got his ear chewed off for it by the matron! Later I apologised personally to the matron. She was very nice about it and it made me realise how much support I have. Also, provided it is not detrimental to clients, it is not the end of the world if you make a wrong decision so long as you learn from it and don't make the same mistake next time. The day ended with a sense of achievement.

Evaluating growth

Both Jenny and Sue used their diaries to chart progress and to identify what they had learnt. This sort of self-knowledge will help both of them in their personal, professional and academic development.

When diary-keeping is combined with goal-setting it is possible to evaluate progress that has been made. Imagine you are Misha. You have analysed what happened and you want to be sure that you have used the experience to ensure that you deal with similar problems more appropriately in future. You approach your manager and discuss setting a goal specifically related to the way in which you manage interpersonal problems. Your goal reads:

Goal statement with timescale:

- Improve, over the next three months, interpersonal skills when dealing with standards of work of staff for whom I am responsible.

Criteria:

Agreed with, and to be assessed by, my manager:

- I am able to bring about improvement in standards without antagonising staff

Action plans:

- Use Val, who is generally held to be exceptionally good at this sort of management, as a role model

- Go to the library and search for at least two books on the subject to read

- Have a discussion with staff on how they prefer to have the need to improve standards addressed.

Your diary will record your discussions with your manager, the way in which you work through your action plans, and the analysis of any situations that occur in which you have to take action on standards.

In this way you will monitor your progress on the action plan and record the achievement of your goal. You can evaluate the whole learning experience by analysing what you have achieved and whether you feel it was worth the effort you put into it. Then, like Misha, you will have made real progress, and you will know exactly what that progress is and how it has been achieved.

Critical-incident analysis, reflective practice and the use of a reflective diary, tied in with a process of goal-setting, will combine to support and monitor your personal and professional growth. This process is far more positive than simply hoping that you have improved in some undefined or loosely expressed way and hoping your manager has noticed it. It ties in with the subject of our next chapter, 'Making the best of assessment'.

5: Making the best of assessment

IN THIS CHAPTER WE SHALL:

- **Describe a range of assessment methods**
- **Consider how you can demonstrate your learning to best advantage**

Who assesses what, and why?

Who and what

Many aspects of our lives are subject to a dual system of assessment. We may assess ourselves and others may assess us. Take preparing a meal as an example:

> I consider that, to be a success, a meal should smell good, look good by being served at an attractively set table, taste good, and be nutritious but low in calories. That's what I am aiming for when preparing a meal for myself.
>
> My son hates cooking, but now that he has his own flat he has to cook for himself. For him a successful meal means filling his stomach as quickly and as cheaply as possible, usually with a 'fry-up', and having only one plate to wash up afterwards.

Clearly, my son and I are looking at different aspects of eating when we assess a meal, and will apply different standards when making our judgements. If we each assess the meals the other prepares, my son will accuse me of starving him and I will probably accuse him of leading me into obesity. So 'who' assesses 'what' can lead to marked differences in judgements.

The same things apply when assessing learning. You, as a student, may assess different things from the items assessed by your tutor. Even if both assess the same items, you may use different standards. That is one of the main problems for students who are being assessed. Open learning is a great help here, particularly if you use a goal-setting process, because the criteria for success are known by the student, and agreed with the supervisor.

The 'why' of assessment

In our example of preparing a meal, we were highlighting the difference between self-assessment and assessment by another person who may have different standards. The problems increase when different people have different reasons for assessing the same item. When my son and I assess each other's meals we will have fairly superficial social reasons for doing so — though in both cases we might claim it was the desire for self-preservation.

If, on the other hand, we were students on a formal catering course, assessment would be carried out for different reasons:

- To provide feedback to each student as part of the learning process. This is known as '*formative*' assessment, because it helps in the formation of knowledge, skills and attitudes

- To measure achievement. This is known as '*summative*' assessment because it is used to 'sum up' the progress made. Summative assessment is often linked to a pass or fail mark and can take place at intervals throughout a course or as a final hurdle at the end.

As a student you are entitled to know exactly what aspects of your progress are being assessed, who is assessing you, what criteria are being used and whether assessments are formative or summative.

Assessment methods

The most commonly used methods of assessing progress are

- Individual performance review

- Project work

- Submitted essays

- Formal examinations.

We will look at them in turn and consider how you can use each of them to your best advantage. If, as you read this section, you decide that you need further help in particular areas, you will find the further reading list at the end of the book offers suggestions for developing the required skills.

Individual performance review

Individual performance review (IPR) is a system where a manager and an employee systematically appraise all aspects of the employee's work performance. Additionally, the employee appraises the way in which the manager's input has influenced performance at work.

You might be surprised to find IPR included in a book for students. However, IPR which results in the identification of skills that could be developed, or of areas of performance which could be improved by study, is very likely to lead to study. Perhaps that is how you came to consider becoming an open learning student. If that is so, or if you simply have a system of IPR where you work, you can prepare now to present your open learning studies in your next IPR.

In Chapter 2 we described the process of goal-setting, with the agreement of measurable criteria for achieving each goal and the identification of appropriate action plans to help you to reach them. We saw how the process can be used to help achieve professional competences, and suggested that each practice-related, or professional, goal and its criteria are agreed with your practice supervisor or tutor. Note is made in the criteria section of who will be involved in assessing when you achieve each competence-related goal.

In this situation you are both quite clear about

- Who the people doing the assessing are — you and your practice supervisor or tutor

- What is being assessed — the goal

- How assessment is being carried out — using the criteria you have agreed.

Where goal-setting is related to IPR, you may find that you achieve some goals before your next scheduled performance review. Informal discussions between you and your manager may acknowledge this and lead to your setting further goals in an ongoing process. At your next formal IPR you will have a lot of progress to review, all of it clearly stated and documented to cheer both you and your manager, who can also see the result of the support he or she has given you.

IPR can therefore be a very constructive element in the life of an open learning student.

Project work

Why do people who design courses often require students to undertake project work? Projects can offer an opportunity for you to:

- Develop additional skills, such as carrying out a literature search and academic writing

- Pursue a topic related to your studies and of particular interest to you

- Investigate a subject and apply what you learn to your own area of work or practice

- Be credited with knowledge and skills that would not be appraised in other types of course work or examination.

If you have to undertake a project you should think through the following points:

Choosing the right topic is vital. It is important to choose something that really interests you because, by the end of it, even the wildest enthusiasm may have waned. If you start off only half committed, your interest will have died long before the end.

Agree the topic subject, and the breadth and depth in which you will cover it, with your tutor. You might find tarantulas endearing creatures and be able to make a good case for using them as the main topic for a project on 'Enhancing the environment' but your tutor may have a broader study in mind. If you persist in working on a project your tutor believes will not offer you the opportunity to achieve the standard of work required, you have only yourself to blame if you do badly in the end.

Obtain information on the criteria by which your project will be assessed. If you find them difficult to understand discuss them with your tutor.

Decide on a suitable structure. Your tutor may give you guidelines on how to approach your project, covering such details as whether you should submit it in stages and whether assessment will be formative or summative. You should also receive some guidance on the length of the completed project and how long you have to do it.

Draw up a project timetable, setting dates by which you intend to have reached certain stages. You are unlikely to do yourself justice if you leave yourself only three days to put together a project which is designed to take three months.

Reference your work. Whenever you refer, in academic work, to ideas or arguments put forward by someone else, you must reference them. Referencing is essential in order to credit other people with the ideas and arguments they have put forward so that you do not appear to be claiming them as your own original thoughts. Additionally, clear referencing allows other people, in this case the person assessing your work, to follow up your references easily and to see that you have analysed and criticised other people's ideas and arguments effectively. Referencing saves us all from making wild and unsubstantiated claims in academic work.

There are a number of acceptable ways of referencing. You may, for example, in discussing multicultural health care, refer as follows:

Leininger has described the aim of transcultural nursing as being to provide care that is as congruent as possible with the clients' cultural values, norms and practices (Leininger, M., 1978).

Alternatively, you could quote Leininger directly, including the number of the page on which the quote appears:

'The aim of transcultural nursing is to provide care that is as congruent as possible with the clients' cultural values, norms and practices' (Leininger, M., 1978, p.158).

In either case you should then list all your references at the end of your written work, in alphabetical order, giving for a book:
— Author's (or authoring editor's) surname and initials
— Year of publication
— Title of the book (usually underlined)
— Place of publication
— Name of publisher

Our example would read:

Leininger, M. (Ed) 1978. *Transcultural Nursing. Concepts, theories and practices.* New York, John Wiley.

In some instances, you may wish to insert the page number.

If your reference is to an article in a journal you should give:
— Author's surname and initials

— Title of the article
— Name of the journal (usually underlined)
— Year of publication
— Volume number of the journal
— Issue number of the journal
— Numbers of the first and last pages of the article.

For example:

Gooch, S. Healthy options. *Nursing Times* 1993; **89**; 8, 41-43.

Take time and trouble in preparing your project for submission. It is only human for an assessor to feel more kindly disposed towards a project that is clearly set out, and presented on nice clean pages in a suitable file or binding, than one which arrives as loose, tatty sheets with the remains of snacks and beverages splattered all over them.

Submitted essays

Have you ever made something from scratch, such as a new garden, without spending sufficient time designing and planning what you intend to do? If you have, you may have laid a new lawn and put bedding plants in new flower beds before realising that you had left yourself nowhere to put the earth you still had to dig out for the fish pond. Hiring a skip to get rid of the excess soil will cost a great deal, and could have been prevented by planning earlier to incorporate it in a raised flower bed. Planning helps to prevent a multitude of disasters and saves a great deal of time in the long run. Essays are just the same. They need careful planning before you start writing, or you may make many disastrous and time-wasting attempts at getting them right. You may also end up submitting a poor essay.

Making an essay plan

The first thing to do is to examine the essay title carefully, underlining key words to clarify what you are expected to write about. Here is an example:

Discuss the *merits* and *disadvantages* of *banning private cars* from city *centres*.

It is obvious that you are expected to write a balanced critique of the good things and the bad things that might result from stopping private citizens taking their cars into the centre of any city. Not just your city, if you happen to live in one, not just London, Glasgow, Belfast or Cardiff, but any city centre. Additionally, although you may put forward your own opinion in the conclusion of your essay, you are expected to present a balanced picture by giving both 'merits' and 'disadvantages'.

Once you are clear about the essay's subject, you have to map out a structure for it. The first paragraph should describe the main points that will be covered in the essay. Subsequent paragraphs will usually each discuss one major point, although if an essay covers only a small number of major points, each one may then be dealt with in a number of paragraphs. Common sense will decide which approach is required. The final paragraph summarises the essay and reaches a conclusion. The plan for this essay might read as follows:

Paragraph 1: Introduction to essay, stating that there are a number of conflicting merits and disadvantages which will be discussed.

Paragraph 2: Major benefit of banning private cars: reduction in air pollution. Briefly describe short- and long- term health dangers of air pollution.

Paragraph 3: Air pollution could be reduced by encouraging car-sharing and by the development and use of electric-powered cars.

Paragraph 4: Second major benefit: commercial and public transport could then flow more freely.

Paragraph 5: Major disadvantages may be that the cost of using public transport might discourage people from coming into city centres, thereby causing centres to 'die'.

Paragraph 6: Third major benefit of banning cars: safer environment for pedestrians.

Paragraph 7: Disadvantage is that many people dislike walking, or are unable to walk, long distances. But pedestrian safety could be increased, and distances reduced, by creating pedestrian precincts.

Paragraph 8: Summarise the arguments for and against and reach a conclusion on the evidence presented in the preceding paragraphs.

How much detail you put into an essay will depend on the academic level at which it is being written, and the reason for writing it. If our example was being written by a student on a general studies college course, that level of content would be adequate. If the student was studying urban planning, much more detail would be required and the essay would have to be widely referenced.

Always write clearly, using simple language and without trying to impress the examiner with unusual or unnecessarily long words. You have time to 'polish' a submitted essay. Consequently, you will be expected to ensure that there are no spelling mistakes, that it is legible and well presented.

Formal examinations

Examinations are a battle of wits in which you set out to provide the examiner with evidence of your knowledge, skills and appropriate attitudes. Although you may have studied a wide range of topics from a variety of angles, it is likely that the examination will focus on key areas.

The wise student tries to work out what the key areas are, and concentrates most revision time on them. Past examination papers may provide some clues, as long as the curriculum has not changed. Your tutor will also be able to guide you. Once you have a list of key areas, draw up a revision timetable and stick to it. In this way you won't try to cram all your revision into the last 24 hours. It is also sensible to avoid exhausting yourself with midnight study the night before the exam.

Try out a wide range of revision techniques, including the flash cards and audio tapes described in Chapter 3. Some people find that playing background music as they record revision tapes helps stimulate the memory. The mere thought of that particular piece of music will in future act as a 'trigger' to unlock the associated knowledge. Replay the music in your head and you will, hopefully, replay the information.

What level of information will your examiner require you to put into the paper? Here is one student's experience.

Carol was a health-care practitioner who was studying for a higher award. One examination paper concerned clinical practice but, although Carol excelled at her clinical work, she failed the paper. Her supervisor was mystified and recommended that Carol talk to someone who had passed the paper and compare notes. Finding that they had answered the same questions, the successful candidate listed all the items she had included in each question. Carol was amazed. 'But they would know I know all that,' she said. 'Surely there is no need to put it all in!'

Carol should have put all the information in her answers. An examiner can know only the things about your knowledge, skills, and attitudes that you show in the examination. It really is a question of writing down, or in an oral or practical assessment, telling or showing the examiners, all that they should know about your knowledge, skills or attitudes, even the things that appear to you to be blindingly obvious. As in a court of law, if you don't offer adequate evidence to support your claims you cannot hope for a judgement in your favour. The basic rule for passing any examination is therefore:

- Offer appropriate and adequate evidence.

You should also be sure that you

- Explain yourself, and write, clearly. Evidence can be taken into account only if it can be read and understood

- Answer the required number of questions. If you are asked to answer four questions, each will carry 25% of the total marks for the paper. If you attempt only three questions you are down to a possible maximum of 75% even if you get full marks for each question. Few of us do that and our chances of failing are much greater if we don't answer the full number of questions. You need to drop only nine marks on each question, going down to 16 for each one — an apparently reasonable mark — to take your total marks below 50%. If that is the pass mark, you will have failed

- Take 10 minutes off the total examination time to allow 'reading through' time at the end and then divide the remaining time by the number of questions you must answer. Use only that time for each question

- Where your answers are required in essay form, use the first five minutes of each question's allotted time to plan your answer, as for a submitted essay

- Read through your answer paper in the final 10 minutes, making sure that sentences make sense and that you have not omitted a vital piece of information. And don't panic. Most of us know more than we give ourselves credit for!

In our final chapter we shall consider how we can measure the educational process as a whole — a much broader undertaking than the learning assessment methods we have discussed here.

6: Evaluating the experience

IN THIS CHAPTER WE SHALL:

- **Describe the process of educational evaluation**
- **Discuss constructive ways of reviewing your diary**
- **Consider the continuing reassessment of goals**
- **Suggest ways in which you can give constructive feedback on educational provision and processes**

Educational evaluation

The term 'assessment' and 'evaluation' are often used interchangeably in everyday language but educationists usually use them very specifically. The term 'assessment' describes the processes, discussed in the previous chapter, by which students' intellectual and practical knowledge, skills and attitudes are measured. The term 'evaluation' is used to describe a process which seeks to answer questions about educational provision. That could be an entire national curriculum, an individual course, one component of a course or an isolated educational experience. The questions are:

- *Is the educational provision effective?* Is the course or other educational provision necessary and appropriate: is it meeting a need?

- *Is it efficient?* Is it producing the best possible educational outcome with the least waste of effort for all concerned?

- *Is it economic?* Is it achieving a successful educational outcome with the minimum possible cost?

You will no doubt be familiar with these kinds of questions in many other aspects of life, from selecting a new vacuum cleaner to looking at how your team at work performs. It makes sense to evaluate any enterprise. In educational evaluation we need to consider all the factors that contribute to, or have a negative effect on, a learning process — the *'inputs'*. We must also measure all the learning, intended or unintended, that has resulted — the '*outputs*'. Viewed together the inputs and outputs will answer the question 'What is happening, or has happened, here?'

As an open learning student your views are not only as valid as those of college principals, tutors or practice supervisors, but they are also central to the whole process of evaluation of any course of study you take. There are a number of ways in which you can approach the process of evaluating your open learning experience. Many of them are, of course, closely related to the assessment of learning because students' assessment is a major element in educational evaluation.

Some aspects of evaluation of a learning experience will provide feedback for you as a student to use in your continuing education, for example evaluating learning methods and assessment strategies. Evaluation of these aspects will help you to make reasoned choices about future methods of study and on the use of self-assessment. Others, such as the usefulness of study materials, and the benefits or otherwise of tutorial support, will offer valuable feedback for those who designed, provided or supported the educational processes in which you have been involved. All will contribute to evaluating your educational experience as a whole.

Reviewing your diary

Educational evaluation should not, however, be a one-off event, undertaken at the end of a course or particular period of learning. Just as assessment should have formative elements to provide continuous feedback, as well as summative elements to measure outcomes at particular stages, so evaluation should include both ongoing monitoring of the learning provision and processes as well as a concluding measurement of all the inputs and outcomes. Your diary is central to this undertaking.

Day-to-day review

In Chapter 4 we discussed the benefits of keeping a reflective diary. In the short term you can gain a great deal from using your diary to analyse critical incidents and from linking such analysis to goal-setting. As you identify action plans to achieve goals you are constantly developing your own individual learning processes.

In the short term you may be able to see evidence of self-development in many areas of your life. Your diary may record dramatic changes in your approach to particular situations, as Sue's did when she realised that making a mistake when first taking charge was not the end of the world. Reflecting on what had happened gave her an appreciation of the support that she had previously taken for granted and also gave her confidence that she could cope even when things did not go according to plan.

Periodic review

In the longer term, reviewing your diary can help you to chart less dramatic but equally fundamental changes in your knowledge, skills and attitudes. This excerpt is, again, a genuine entry from the reflective diary of an open-learning student, Anne, who is nearing the completion of a professional development course.

> 2/10. What a reward. I am the mentor for our new care assistant. I am helping her to learn and meet her job description. It seemed so natural to use the goal-setting process as I myself did. I feel very valuable and knowledgeable; she's a lovely lady who is so enthusiastic. I really feel I can help her now to build a foundation for the future — she is developing a professional profile.

Anne has identified her new skills of profiling and goal-setting as applying not only to her own ongoing development but also to her new role as a mentor.

Reassessing goals

Because she has transferred the new skills to a different role Anne will have a different part to play. In the goal-setting process Anne will now take the 'expert' role in agreeing criteria for the achievement of her care assistant's goals. She may feel that she should set herself new goals to develop this new role.

Because Anne completed a personal and professional profile, has kept a reflective diary, and has used a goal-setting process, she has a clear record of her progress over the months she has been a student on her course. Using these processes has enabled her to:

- Identify her strengths and her areas for growth

- Set goals for personal and professional development

- Analyse critical incidents

- Chart her progress using those critical-incident analyses, general reflection and the specific goal-setting process.

Will she put her profile, her diary and her goal file away at the end of her course?

Where do I go from here? My diary is evidence that I am not the same person I was even six months ago: I have changed so much. I find that thinking in an objective way is second nature to me now. I will re-profile myself within one month of completing my course, decide where I want to go from here and set myself new personal and professional goals.

In reaching that conclusion Anne has recognised that profiling, reflective diary-keeping and goal-setting can be continuing processes in her life, and that she will use them to continue her personal growth.

Evaluating educational experiences generally

In addition to using continuing evaluation of personal outcomes from educational processes, we should all play a part in providing feedback on educational provision.

Giving constructive feedback

Because you are an open learning student your views will be sought for a number of reasons:

Concern for other students. If you have found part or all of a course to be faulty in some way, it is unlikely to be altered unless the faults are brought to the attention of those with the power to bring about improvement. If that is not done, other students will continue to suffer inadequate educational provision or processes.

Tutors need feedback on the usefulness of their teaching input. Although genuinely committed to helping you to learn, tutors may have failed to identify learning needs, have used unhelpful teaching methods or failed to give adequate feedback to help you learn. Unless you tell them in which areas they could improve, they are unlikely to be able to do so. Tutors who have previously worked in closed learning environments may also need your feedback to encourage them to have confidence in their new open approach. Additionally, where study materials are used, the people who design and produce the materials, your 'tutors-in-text', need ongoing feedback to help them update those materials and produce new units and courses.

Peers (your fellow students or colleagues), practice supervisors and managers may, like tutors, be totally committed to supporting your learning, but may put limits on your learning by misinterpreting the support you require. Unless you tell them, they will not know. Where you can tell them that their support has been invaluable they will be encouraged to extend their skills to supporting others.

Educational establishments spend vast amounts of money planning courses, buying materials, employing tutors and organising support for students. In the majority of cases the money that they spend comes out of your pocket, either directly because as a student you pay your fees, or indirectly in the form of taxes. Do you want your money to be wasted? Unless you provide feedback to colleagues and other educational establishments, directors and staff will be deprived of vital information on the wisdom of spending funding in particular ways. If they have no positive feedback on a course, they may even discontinue what is actually seen by students to be very useful.

In evaluating a particular educational experience you therefore need to provide feedback on:

- Course provision — was this/another course needed?

- Course design — was the learning process/content/assessment appropriate?

- Tutorial input — did it meet your needs?

- Managerial support — was it appropriate and adequate?

- Practice supervision — did it assist learning?

- Peer support — were you enabled to help each other?

If you are provided with feedback forms, do fill them in and return them promptly so that they can be acted on immediately. If you are not asked to provide feedback, use your reflective diary to identify aspects of your student experiences on which it would be helpful to provide feedback. Take the initiative and offer your constructive evaluation.

You need to identify:

- What you think it is important to provide feedback about

- Why you think it is important to provide feedback on this particular aspect

- To whom you will give feedback

- What you hope to achieve.

Positive aspects

You need to provide feedback sensitively and to highlight positive aspects of educational provision and support as well as less satisfactory experiences. In Chapter 4 we quoted Sue's experience of being in charge on operations day and her realisation of the tremendous support she received in her workplace. Although Sue's diary does not record that she told her peers and managers how much she appreciated their support, they would no doubt have been grateful for, and have benefited from, such feedback.

In summary, the crucial factors about educational evaluation are that it should:

- Be fair and objective, rather than biased and emotional

- Identify good, as well as encouraging revision of inadequate or inappropriate, educational provision or teaching

- Be addressed to the people who are in a position to act upon it

- Be made with due regard for the feelings of others.

Which brings us back to you. By now you probably have little doubt that being an open learning student is likely to become a lifelong process. The first bookworm was undoubtedly an open learning student, eating his educational way into everyday language. Who knows what your academic future holds? Good luck with your studies, and remember — **you are in charge**.

REFERENCES

1 Lewis, R. What is open learning? *Open Learning* 1986; **1**: 2. 5-10.
2 Keegan, D. *The Foundations of Distance Education.* London: Croom Helm, 1986.
3 Carpenter, D. Advocacy. The 'how' of advocacy. Unit 9 (ii). *Professional Development. A continuing education module for nurses.* London: Macmillan Magazines, 1993, 157–163.
4 Adams, J. Human Biography. A personal approach. Unit 2 (i). *Professional Development. A continuing education module for nurses.* London: Macmillan Magazines, 1993, 32–38.
5 *The Open Learning Directory.* Oxford: Pergamon Open Learning, 1997.
6 Student Research Centre, Institute of Educational Technology, Open University. The human dimension in open university study. *Open Learning* 1986; **1**: 2; 1-17.
7 Emap Healthcare Open Learning. The Profile Pack. London: Emap Healthcare Ltd, 1998.
8 Handy, C. *Inside Organisations.* London: BBC Books, 1990.
9 Schön, D. *The Reflective Practitioner. How professionals think in action.* Aldershot, Hants: Avebury Press, 1991, 299.

• *The Macmillan Publications listed above are now available from Emap Healthcare Open Learning. For more information call our hotline: 020 7874 0600.*

FURTHER READING

Bisset, D. A. student's view of distance learning. *Nursing* 1990; 4: 8, 13-14.
A refreshingly direct account of what it is like to study on a distance learning course, with some practical hints on how to survive.

McSweeney, P. How to conduct a literature search. *Nursing* 1990, 4: 3, 19-22.
The author offers a practical way to search nursing literature and then how to make an effective record of what you have learnt.

Northedge, A. *The Good Study Guide.* Milton Keynes: The Open University, 1990.
Contains a wealth of detailed information for the student who requires more study skills updating than there is room for in this open learning student's guide. Chapter 5 on essay writing is particularly helpful.

Owen, D., Davis M. *Help With Your Project. A guide for students of health care.* London: Edward Arnold, 1991.
Designed to help students identify and undertake a simple project. Although the examples relate to health care, the text readily transfers to other fields.

Robinson, K. M. *Open and Distance Learning for Nurses.* London: Longman, 1989.
A very useful introduction to open and distance learning approaches. Although aimed specifically at nurses, the book contains much of interest and help to others.

Rowntree, D. *Learn How to Study: A guide for students of all ages* (3rd edition). London: Macdonald Orbis, 1988.
An easy-to-digest, practical guide to study techniques.

Other study materials published by Emap Healthcare Open Learning are:

Study Skills For Adult Learners, Karen Rawlins, 1996
Study Guides: Your Guide to Essential Study Skills, Karen Rawlins and
    Diane West
Presentation and Communication Skills: A Handbook for Practitioners.
    Karen Rawlins, 1996
Profiles and Portfolios: A Guide for Nurses and Midwives, Cathy Hull
    and Liz Redfern, Macmillan Press, 1996.

For more information, contact:

Emap Healthcare Open Learning
Emap Healthcare Ltd
Greater London House
Hampstead Road
London NW1 7EJ
Tel: 020 7874 0600
Fax: 020 7874 0601